HOUSE MADE OF SILVER

ELIZABETH
ROBINSON

KELSEY ST PRESS

For Chris
& Mary
(an older book)
yours,
Elizabeth

ACKNOWLEDGMENTS

The author would like to thank the magazine and chapbook editors of the following for their support in the publication of some of these poems: *Avec; Apex of the M; Black Fire, White Fire; Brief; Chain; Furnitures; Oblek*. "Nearings" and "Iemanje" previously appeared in eponymous chapbooks published by Leave Books and Meow Press respectively. I would also like to thank the Fund for Poetry and the MacDowell Colony for support which made the writing of many of these poems possible. Their support is deeply appreciated. Finally, my appreciation to Patricia Dienstfrey for a particularly attentive and helpful reading of these poems.

Publication of this book was made possible by a grant from the California Arts Council.

Library of Congress Cataloging-in-Publication Data

Robinson, Elizabeth, 1961–
     House made of silver / by Elizabeth Robinson.
        p. cm.
     ISBN 0-932716-51-2
     I. Title.
     PS3568.O2883 H68 2000
     811'.54—dc21   00-043573

Book Design by Mark Fox and Scott Gagner / BlackDog

All orders to: Small Press Distribution
                    800-869-7553 email: orders@spdbooks.org
Visit Kelsey St. Press online at: www.kelseyst.com

This book is for Avery, Drew, and George.

CONTENTS

ITS EXCESS

Tea swaying in its cup
and someday
all over

red and menthol
samples of life laying themselves
on our table

And then
windows cleaned at night
by the light of an onion dome
will show

no burnish marks

You wake
bared in your fingers
fortuitous and extra
our
emphasis

ITS COMPANION

Ties the leaf,
a thread

of what denomination

of

breath

Finally a visible soul in history

Delivery

sucked from its outbranching and tissue
The length of a stride

so exhausts
what it wants

What

a world this compassed ether
emits

Slow
sniffing at amnesia,

brushing
a series of clumsy reports

On a map sewn with leaves, all

surrounding   A Succor
wrapped

in string, it must
be opened for the mouth   Short

of air
its tie

IEMANJE

i.

As under sound

The seeming presence

I clatter

bent on chipping color

pretense I ingest

ii.

An evil

good—

one or

more iris, pocket

spread, suing

Time

unelected

iii.

This lightness

all its dirt

noise and violence

Scooping up

the hidden hand

a renewal of matches

mis-stayed

iv.

Then, again, entirely sullen

warmth that pulls

that hair

from this mouth

A birthday

or suspicion

pursing its gift

v.

Having stolen

the walking one

leaking gold, stilts

or the uncalled for

right to design

and laundering, to abolish and

watch the turgid air

vi.

Work of preservation

in winter

Hood unheard of, ranges

Inoculate

Be imperious

or cross back

to it, always penultimate

vii.

Looking in their quarters

for that highest ceiling   A skirt

picturing us

The bareheaded

giving off

the movement for beacons

FOR RAIN

i.

Nothing protects so well as this porousness.
A bright deterrent.
A color of sponge, aside.

No, correction:
measure this stride
which would be true.

Would will itself.

ii.

Then there is certainty
this would generate.
Of its lowering:

lit concrete
made wet.

      Overarching what's
brought, not yet
easily pervaded.

iii.

Caused to hesitate, only

clatter borne,

only, that directs, cloudily,
upsurge. Despite.

iv.

Nothing discloses this shelter,

lent a way.

All that steps swallow
to imprint its steady receipt.

NEARINGS

i.

Call out the first name:

a rock flew
it penetrated carbon

Conquering
conquering
the window

And waking early
for lack of memory

Liking the unwaking word

of the holy picture

Stood sentry
twice as many times the "I" of it

Was a frame
when the heart leapt

ii.

Never to have seen
foam as hers means   consecrated

to God
of the rugged

The sea the crumbs
blistering the dark

Commissioned at an early age
to make the oil of sainthood

Nonsense preceding

vast stuttering
and blinking

below which he fiddled

Kindly

iii.

Dropping
the lighter feet, and bare

As an animal would have teased
and shivered and

backed off   Why
is this one

all
the gluey bread that clings at mouth

the dialogue

What sort

of conqueror
His new clothes

iv.

These are the small hands
of having been outdone

A communal shower
sired

that rain was indiscretion
The page's impression

v.

A wrestler
and visited by the lake

Without which spectacles one could not see

Shored up

this seed for bread put in sand
stranded in voice

Gets up at noon
and then rows

vi.

This adds
This page

Be born out of

Wake up mid
I saw a funnel

up there
the other name was
guardian
guardian

Then it went away in the color

RETURN

i.

One

who would be you
brought hand over hand

under water

Distant from advent
or any sense

But still there are
lilies   Your hands
submerged

ii.

Beneath that fluid border
one has to

prepare for the responsibility of presence

A fig tree blown over in a storm
is still milky

with sweetness   That deaf applause

by which hands raise

and flutter

iii.

I see your caress in its basin

whereas I

blow air from my mouth
to warm up cold fingers

All gesture is it
that walks around
the haven

I repeat my selfhood endlessly
but there are still blotches

much lower
in the sink

all those fallen petals
demolishing the floor

iv.

A harrowing

already I'm depleted of experience

Preparation, is it
the reverse

after waiting so long
and turning the faucet

As though swimming were a solution
so harsh on the water

v.

This much changes by the end of the day
a form of taxation

its deafness melodic and
its staining pollen

not rinsable
but like

the anniversary of a birth

vi.

I understand how they would warp and soften

Your fingers under water so long
by now

I begin to hover in your name
at its midpoint

TERM

i.

House
hung by a blue string

The edge of a three leaf

table

of light
The eye's

reversal of showering bits
of the word you wish to join:

House made of pewter
and
House made of silver

ii.

You crack at
the shell

of a supposed egg asking
that its partitioned fruit

be the repository of many entries

iii.

The brick floor from which the
kingdom of God extends

or could extend

This is the hard table

with the door-like segments of its foldings

iv.

compared to the spine
of her leaning over it

A house swung from the neck,

its meteor shower
full of isolated eyes

This, not suspended
but tinted in itself and

blue breaking between
its separate floors

Addendum to the table
always

flattening more perfectly
in its service

TO RE S/VOLVE

i.

Traveling through the
desert
in a silent vehicle

Remember that

Secret knowledge

Not

of light
but of light's
movement

The vehicle
did not lack
yet did not have

purpose
In the light's
mute foresight

I saw

apparently
to sustain
the furled road

ii.

Huffed through
the loose fabric

Condensation on
the vessel that was

not a glass

Clothing always
by contraries

A wry breastplate
(an x-ray)

now pried free
of its ostensible
subject

Not yet though
a product

of transparency

My partiality
errant

iii.

A very brief—

interrupted—

a very scant

term of humility

I'm shaken off
in departure

Sandaled in
speech

and willing
to sing

For there is
after all a document

that bares and
shields the feet

Willing it

To wait

iv.

Will he retrieve for me
what I want

Frippery
Impossible girdling

of a realm

A sash on the fire
claims its holy

superfluity

Look back
on what you were

So naturally
dissimilar and like

I was

Those distinctions
the very basis

of the day's fertility

v.

"This is the mark
in every letter of mine."

Phoneme, not epistle

"It is the way I write."
Helmet

gilded in an old
innocence

Sprays of
vegetation

issue forth,
distort the face

Enhance vision
It is a mode

never aggressive,

made and meant
to distinguish

vi.

Veiled or broken
but both pleasing

And a thing that
once seemed
not to work

took so little
alteration

Sniff at it
How I luxuriate

in my own
odd wardrobe

Single, but not
quite so lone

as to repudiate
its suspension:

"I feel a divine
jealousy for you."

SITE LEGEND

After
all the effort
to scale down the sense of fit, say,
to the size of a human,
whoever she might be.

. . .

Maps are for
the badly behaved.
Stickiness
of the construction
I want to make less petulant.

The presence of glue,
I believe,
forestalls randomness.
No longer
a matter of building
but locating.

Old, overused sites
are forbidden.
The home
would be situated,
ideally,
in the center of the map.

Where am I, as assigned.

. . .

I suspect
we should not
measure with that
image
of the body
as though its terrain
would rest on a self.

Because of this,
a list would not be helpful.
I would forget
how to rummage through
those gestures
I most want to qualify.

I foresee
that things folded up
once were not.

. . .

This is where I am at home,
examining the creases. Otherwise,
we might abet a place
in the guise of a human
who stretches her limbs
over purpose.

There should be many types of fields
clutching their small folds. Shifts
supplanting gestures. Manageable
gestures, how they
refer back to familiar directions.
The arm that points, here,
is not habitual but genuine.

THE FERRY
for Cole Swenson

i.

Let's begin again.
A storybook
on a raft,

this unattributable gift
by comparison.

The black tabling surface
between the self and God

assumes the shape,
half a room over,
of a child.

Whom would you love,
a child
or the possibility of conflicting lights

which offer rest?

Administer, they say,
a heaping teaspoonful, an antidote.

ii.

Some things about myself
I would be able to smell anywhere.

The span between the table and
the wall

in the shape of a couple,
arms around each other.

God would divide the original cell
of twins,

these ones,

smelling the range of distances.

I would be one of two twins

who loves this image of God.

iii.

You hear water running
and the hunch of a shape.

Shape's intention as measurement:

and the domestic storybook shows
God baking a pie

so that when the oven door shuts,
its light goes out.

iv.

Would you love your alarm clock
which wakes you.

Would you love your twinned daughter.

I would love to read the story of
these vagabonds adrift on a raft,

so insubstantial,
who built a sink

aboard
so they could wash in seawater

and keep sanctity.

v.

Half way.

Lights so perturbed with each other
that they expand the presence of God.

Barely. The children playing
in the street are going blind.

These invocations are roughly
the same as sleep

disturbed again by the youngest
who's woken from a bad dream.

From here to there an antidote.

CREASES

i.

And quilt through recall
the intertwined star, slept

boxes of it

as though it were
a blanket on the reverse

an ant   climbing the wall

Lord
of skin
and clashing pattern

Mounds of rags
one two three

four five six three

like the thud
of balm and

on the floor
even worse

when he called
fanning

a green dress
to relax one's muscles
not recounting what the nearly almighty has done

.

ii.

A copy

in the eye of the Lord

growing ready
So I fell asleep again
head above the oscillation

Buds in the star, say,

shot through with house lamps

botched the wall

Flowers walling back feathers

Ripe Lord folded four times in two drawers

iii.

Having the fine hair to resume

Chaotic stripes
and one

no replies

where the antennae wear out

Ruler on the seam of the pillow
by token
of faith

slept
clad

Bifurcate body of peace

iv.

Wreath of blond birds

whom the Lord calls
indigestible
disengaged

Myself by this one

I accuse

down upside flight

v.

Circular pillow
source for provision

I embroider with mature stock

handles on green clothes
remiss in authority

This is a One
with a texture

in all things between skin

and cotton   An ant
and a plasterer

who calls me Effective

white
and blue
by my climbing

vi.

Nub and lint

the relief

I accuse

flies

Rejoinder

susceptible to the fingering

vii.

Who is the maker of the signature

and garb

driving through shade

Effective again
and quelling

In this, one's portability
the smell of feathers

pulled up from underneath

EMITTED ADORATION

i.

Upended the bosom that
the vase made.

Supplicant,
you repeat yourself.

A snag on the bedding
on the base

mutes the color
where it was forced to kneel.

ii.

Who hid an infant in the oval
where fleshes combined.

But who
had ridden the memory

to this joint.

You repeat yourself,
repeat

a whitening

that yields, not gladly.

It was color again,
was incontinent,

who stained the floor.

Had something to ask.

iii.

A sort of fury
that whitewashed the

window's opening.

A sort of gratitude,
chalky as teeth.

Muteness.

I held the bouquet
upside down

and washed it with talc.

Emitted adoration
with all its milky hackles.

What brought back itself,
later, a fit of speechlessness, a gift.
A cluster of benignities.

iv.

Which wheel dissolved
from the cathedral's groin.

Lights   in it

hit like bells
angry for pleasure.

Duel.   Blued.

The sacrament of paper, careful,
that entreats persistence.

v.

Grace is top-heavy,
dead center

before its frame.
Pain was similarly made.

A former fabric was stolen.
Witnessed in a shawl with handles.

Imagined a guardian would adjure.
A guardian whose trueness of blade

would pare
the shield.

Imagination was redundant.
Whittled the stem away to its water.

vi.

The pictures were porous.
I suggested a mantle

and swept away.
Unexpected strength of arm,

so up high
that the lifts returned.

Pictures clung to the sponge.

I suggested a mantle
so little debased

that a satin rolled me over.
Shimmered in the function

it was meant to finish.
Pinpricked a blood sample.

vii.

As Sabbath, metals collect.
Limbs of miracles

forgotten.
Forgot to tell the truth.

A schooling of hands

overflowing with water.
Remembered to replace the clear
with the opaque,
but it was still water.

A memory of the tripartite fold.

viii.

A portion of the cleft brought
by translation.

Angles of the antlers shed
on the breach.

Denies this:

a wrinkle in the filter,
transliteration.

Who was cognate for the organ
of impairment. Who held a spike
—and the tissue—out, until the fibers rattled.

ix.

Could not resist a numbed portion,
the mumbling bit.

Disregard was an infection
that lay itself atop

the image.

The pallor might administer
to its vertices.

This was a politeness, but its vigor
was hidden.

A trick of Lilliputians,
injecting dullness.

x.

Then saw a camera through the pinhole
who stepped double

for every impression.

The single dimension of miracles.
The chain that slings silvered items.

This story is about the surface of the folds.
I hid an envelope underneath the cloth.

Wanted to say so.

xi.

Could will obedience
and that's what the sense
of falling was.

A blue mark in the right hand corner.

Could stutter in the blur.
But mostly, the fact was direct.

The brands of fact to be envisioned in heat.
All this increased.

It buried itself in the area of focus.
A clutching of lips to the impetus.

xii.

Then who saw an image pushing through
the limit of the aperture.

It was the reverse of the prey
who broke its captor's jaw.

Who told the family to move backward, slowly.

Then saw the bunching

of the downward lines. Slightly too much
pressure.

Gray. Protrusion ceased
to deter relief.
But the impasse was blotted out.